T0156990

# WOMEN ARE THE
# NEW MEN

# WOMEN ARE THE NEW MEN

## BUT WHO'S GAMING WHO?

By:

KENNY MACK

iUniverse, Inc.
Bloomington

**Women Are the New Men**
**But Who's Gaming Who?**

*Copyright © 2011 by Kenny Mack.*

*All rights reserved. No part of this book may be used or reproduced by any means, graphic, electronic, or mechanical, including photocopying, recording, taping or by any information storage retrieval system without the written permission of the publisher except in the case of brief quotations embodied in critical articles and reviews.*

*iUniverse books may be ordered through booksellers or by contacting:*

*iUniverse*
*1663 Liberty Drive*
*Bloomington, IN 47403*
*www.iuniverse.com*
*1-800-Authors (1-800-288-4677)*

*Because of the dynamic nature of the Internet, any web addresses or links contained in this book may have changed since publication and may no longer be valid. The views expressed in this work are solely those of the author and do not necessarily reflect the views of the publisher, and the publisher hereby disclaims any responsibility for them.*

*Any people depicted in stock imagery provided by Thinkstock are models, and such images are being used for illustrative purposes only.*
*Certain stock imagery © Thinkstock.*

*ISBN: 978-1-4620-4484-9 (sc)*
*ISBN: 978-1-4620-4482-5 (hc)*
*ISBN: 978-1-4620-4481-8 (ebk)*

*Library of Congress Control Number: 2011914371*

*Printed in the United States of America*

*iUniverse rev. date: 08/29/2011*

# About This Book & The Authors Experiences

This book "Women Are The New Men" shows that women have a hidden power that men often overlook. Men often feel as though we are the species that invented all the tricks and all the game resulting in the female never knowing what hit her until its over. This book will demonstrate time after time that when we as men think we win we really lose.

"Women Are The New Men" takes u through all the stages of the relationship between men and women. It points out how game is used at the beginning of a relationship all the way to the end. Throughout the book readers will discover that men create their own battles that they cannot win. This book highlights some of the most memorable parts of Kenny Mack's life. These experiences have shown him that men have nothing on women when it comes to game.

Focus groups and blog participants also came together to discuss more in depth the dating and relationship concept of game. The heart sometimes thinks for an individuals mind and decisions are made out of love instead of reason. The wants the needs of the heart control our action, and this book puts them all in perspective. The next time those words of a persuasive female touch the ear of men everywhere they will be able to make decisions with their mind not just their heart.

This book is for the man that ever wanted to know what a woman was really thinking when she meets you, kisses you, hugs you, tells you she loves you, or claims that you are her best friend then this is the book for you.

# Chapter 1

# Real Talk (I probably wont trust you)

Super Bowl 1994 I remember begging my mom to let me go watch the game at Sharron's house. I convinced her by saying that there was a large group of us going to watch together. My mom didn't really want to let me go to a female's house but since she is one of the coolest moms in the world, she eventually caved in. The Super Bowl started and we were all into the game until Dallas started beating Buffalo pretty bad. I think the final score was 30 to 13. During the forth quarter I walked off into the computer room. Sharron followed me into the room, and started kissing me. Now Sharron was fine; maybe the prettiest girl on the cheerleader squad. Sharron had thick caramel thighs, soft beautiful eyes and a smile that would stop a deer. Sharron also was a senior and I was in my first year of high school. It wasn't the first time that she and I had kissed, but it was the first time that we had kissed so sexual. As I was sitting on the computer chair she started to grab on my mid section, and the rest is history. I was dumb struck; it felt so good and so real that I just knew I was in love. Sharron and I would stay on the phone until five in the morning, I was at her house after school all the time, and we would skip school together. I was under the impression that she liked me. Sharron spent all of her free time with me either on the phone or skipping class. So

1

when she started kissing me at her house all sexual I had to ask Sharron if she was my girlfriend. She laughed and said "Yeah I will be your girl." I was like, "for real I want you to be my Girl." And she said "yeah baby I am yours for real".

When we got back in school the next day I felt like I was walking on the moon. I had a beautiful girl that I was proud to say was mine. Once I started telling people that Sharron and I were together, they told me when they had slept with her. I was like whoa, when did she have time to have sex with all these people? It didn't matter, because I was still going to have sex with her. At least I thought I was going to be able to still have sex with Sharron!

On Valentine's Day I went to school late with a bunch of balloons, and a big teddy bear for her. She looked shocked when I gave them to her, but she gave me a big kiss and said thank you anyway. I asked her if I could take her out that night and Sharron said that she had some homework to do but she would love to go out that weekend. I was like, cool. I tried to call her that night and her mom answered and said that she wasn't at home. Me being so naive, I said to myself, "maybe she went to a friends house and did her homework". The next day at school I went to the gym and the star basketball player was talking about the date he had with Sharron the night before. Needless to say I was played to the fullest. Sharron had told me that she was my girl for real, she told me that she had home work for real, and she made me feel that I was the only one she wanted in her life. It was a sad day in history for me. She scarred me pretty bad, and made me the way that I am now. I always think the worst, and I always figure someone is trying to run game. So if you say "real talk" I probably won't trust you.

# Chapter 2

# Opening

Game is being able to be smooth with the opposite sex. It's being able to convince someone of something that is far from the truth and being able to persevere through any situations and come out as the winner. The thing about fellas is that we play games and think that we are playing by ourselves. That is, until that day when we are extremely surprised and disappointed to find out the one thing that we had feared about our girl, that she was playing the game too. Games have winners and losers. In a relationship who is the winner who is the loser? The winner is the person that cares the least because they can get over it the fastest. The person that cares the least is able to do what they feel, and do what they want to do and worry about explaining their self at a later date.

Game has been around for a very long time and women have always been the masters of every kind of game. Back in the early 1900's when it was taboo for a woman to have sex with a man that she was not married too (unless she was earning money) women used other ways to exercise their game. Remember the first push up bras? Women would tie those little slips really tight to make their breasts stand up. Their breasts would point out so far that every time a man looked over at her, he thought she was pointing her breasts at him. She would flash a shy smile then look down and away giving him the opportunity to get a look, so that he would want to come meet her. It's just like right now when women leave their house for a party; they look in the mirror and say "I'm getting me a man tonight. I'm wearing my butt jeans and somebody is going to see my ass in these jeans and fall in love". You think they dress like that all the time? Hell no. They only have about five outfits that show off what they think are their best body parts.

One of my ex-girlfriend's had big breasts and some of the best legs; every time we went out together she made sure she showed those parts. Even though she was with me there may have been someone out there that was just a little bit better. That is a woman's game. It's not an accident that you like what you see; every guy in the building likes what he sees. Women are going to play on what men like. This is why it takes them hours to get ready. It is obvious that they have to put all this phony stuff on to make themselves look more attractive. It's called make-up for a reason; they make up how they want to look, and its all game. Once you get the female home you notice that her butt looked and felt a lot bigger in those jeans. Then you're thinking this is some bull, I should have gone home to my wife.

Then there are the desperate women who re-invent themselves to create someone that one may think is fun and different. What women did was they created ways to invite men to have sex with them. It used to be few and far between that you would find a woman that wanted to have sex as soon as you met her, but there were a few. These days the endangered species that was so hard to find is on every corner, in every club, at every church, and some are the big bosses for major corporations. There are women that give head (perform oral sex) on the first night, leave no evidence on the first night, and so many other unmentionable things happen on the first night. They do whatever it takes to stand out from the rest; that's what the fellas and I call hoes. Please don't get me wrong, if you are having sex on the first night, don't stop. The fellas and I love to meet these women; it helps us with our self confidence. It would really be sexy if just for once I had sex with a female on the first night and she didn't say anything stupid like, "you know I normally don't do things like this". I wish just one time a woman would say "you are the fifth one night stand this week". I would probably be scared as hell for about two weeks, until I got the doctors results, but I would respect the fact that she was real.

Sometimes promiscuous women can be intriguing, especially if you've never had a woman that would just wild out for you. Those women are trouble too, they are the ones that you end up spending so much time with because their sex is so crazy and you forget that she is the same person she was before you got there. Sex is just one of the weapons women use to run game, but their most effective weapon is that they understand men, better then we understand women.

My Dad told me one time that "women make it so easy on men now days," that could have went down as the realest words he ever spoke. I was about seventeen, and my friends and I had a bad habit of calling the girls basketball team "Hoes". My dad overheard us saying, "what time the hoe's play", and that's when he said what he said. I remember it like it was yesterday. My Dad said that when he was growing up there was maybe one or two girls that everyone knew was giving it up, but all of the females we had all messed with were open like a 7 Eleven. That was true because all the females that I knew were definitely having sex and it didn't take much to get them.

In one of the focus groups that I held I surveyed a group of women and asked them how many of them had previously had sex on the first night with multiple partners. Surprisingly, on paper 80 percent of the women said they had. Then once we got into the session, and we were all face to face, I asked the same question in a different way. I asked how many of them would have sex with someone that they meet on the first night. I wanted to see if the same amount of women would admit that they would be willing to have first date sex. This time only 45 percent of the room raised their hands. The truth is that women do know what their plans are with you when they first meet you. The only difference is the game that they want to play. They choose from the minute they meet you if they want to sleep with you or not. Women also choose if they think that a man is marriage material, or if you would just be fun to play with for a while. That is why I got those different answers. If you are marriage material, they will play the cat and mouse game when you take them to dinner, movies, bowling and everywhere else for months and they won't have sex with you. Guys think that they have found a different kind of girl, when the truth is that she was having sex with the last guy everyday and he wasn't spending a dime on her. The only reason that she isn't having sex with you is because she sees something different in you. You have a special quality. So she will put on a front and pretends like she had never given it up to anyone, that she wasn't in a serious relationship with. The problem comes in when the guy believes this story is the truth. Fellas look at their pervious relationships and know that it has never taken them this long to have sex with someone, especially when they are throwing out all their tricks to have sex with this woman and none of them are working. What he has failed to notice is the fact that she knows that he has not had to work this hard to get any one female in bed. She is going to use that to her advantage. At the end of your dates when you are trying to get her in bed with you, she is going to say things like, "you must think I'm like all the other girls you been with, if this all you want out of this relationship we can end it now." She knows you are five months in and maybe fifteen movies, twelve dinners, and a vacation, you have spent way too much money to end the relationship that easy. Plus you have invested something greater than money, time. During this time a lot of things have happened. Females bank on this and hope that during this time you have developed an emotional attachment to them. Fellas can say what they want but women know that we are just as emotional as them when it comes to love. During all your dates with her, the time you spent, conversation that you both had, you've built a bond that you are not just going to give up. In her eyes she has to make herself seem extremely respectful or different so that you will want to marry her.

The females that will have sex with you on the first night usually have a boy friend, ex-boy friend or someone that they are already trying to marry, so they see you as a fun toy. Don't think that you are off the hook; they are going to hit you with that game too. They are going to tell you that they have never done anything like this before and you are the first guy that she was ever this attracted too. They say all these things just to make you feel different. Guys tend to believe that they are different, better, and can make any women have sex with them on the first night. Since women are smarter than men they already know how to play on the psyche and ego and still make you feel special. Actually you're no different than the next man that she is going to have sex with on the first night. She boosts your ego just in case so if this one night stand turns into a relationship she has already saved her faced by making you feel different. In this case it all depends on how well you do your job that will determine if you're going to stay around. As boyfriend number two you have an easy task of having really good sex with her. Your job is to break her back. If you can do this she will keep you around for a while. But if you are not any better than the man she is with . . . umm you may get fired before you get that third try. She doesn't want to have a relationship with you because she checking for someone else.

Women never want you to know who they really are. That is why there was such a big difference in the percentage of women that answered the question one way first then flipped their answer in person. It's a little game in everything that a woman does. Then I asked the real question, "when you meet a guy within ten minutes do you know if you will have sex with him or not?" 95 percent of them said yes, and most said it doesn't take that long. So my follow up question was, "if you know you are going to have sex with him, then why make him wait? Why play the game?" All of them said the same thing. They believed that the guy probably wouldn't respect them if they gave it up on the first night.

For women it is all in how you carry yourself, if you keep yourself up, and whom you choose to sleep with. If a woman sleeps with the wrong person, even if it is only one person, she will be known as a whore. If you dress a certain way you are a whore. I don't make the rules I just live by them. When I was young, females would say, "hell I'm young I can do what I want to do." Now that I'm older they say "hell I'm grown and you're grown so lets make it happen". Then in some miraculous way they expect you to respect them and call them the next day.

Well, let me tell you, if a woman gives me head before we go out on a date, what makes them think I would ever respect, or trust her. Everyone makes mistakes but not the same damn mistake over and over and over again. That is why women resort to game. They play games to make you feel sorry, to make you love them, or to make you care. As I got older and started messing with every kind of woman, young, old, and all nationalities I noticed that women have more game than men, so who is gaming who?

One of the biggest differences is that women hold a lot of the responsibility these days too. The days where the man worked and the woman stayed at home to clean and take care of the children are long gone. Now women make just as much money, if not more than their spouse or their boyfriend. So the days where the man could just call and say hey baby I know I said I would be home by six, but I have to work late are long gone and are over. He would show up at twelve at night smelling like another women's perfume and his wife or girlfriend would not say a word because she had no where to go. Now women are the ones making that call, they have just as much power as the man now. Everything is an equal partnership, she is paying half the bills, and she bought half, if not all the things in the home. So if you're going to play the run the street game she is going to play it too.

To admit that you have been played is hard for a man to do because they all have big egos. What you will find throughout this book is that sometimes when you think that you are gaming females they are really gaming you. That is the question that has yet to be answered, but soon will be answered. I'm going to break it down so it can forever and always be broken.

# Chapter 3

## "Who met who"

Game starts from the very beginning. Have your boys ever told you never to trust a chick that you met in the club? Well let me tell you why you shouldn't. You approach a nice looking lady sitting at the bar, you make small conversation and the next thing you know you ask for her number. Now you just bagged that chick and in your heart you feel like you ran game to get her number. The truth is that she saw you an hour ago, she and her friends have been plotting on a way to get her into your line of sight for hours. If you remember she was on the phone when you first spotted her. She was actually having a conversation with her girlfriend who was telling her exactly which way to turn and look so you could see her. As soon as you looked her way she smiled at you giving you the invitation to come over and get her number. That little smile was all it took for your confidence to go from 50 to 100 percent. Women know men and know what we will fall for because we do it all the time. Despite what you felt happened when you got her number, trust and believe that she saw you hours before you ever saw her. She wanted to make you feel like you came on to her. For this reason in the future if you all get into an argument she can always say, "You came on to me. If this isn't what you wanted you should have never came over there and asked for my number, but we are here now so we have to make it work."

I asked a group of single women if when they go to different venues with their friends are they going there to meet someone or to have a good time with their friends? They all lied straight to my face and said that they were going to have fun with their friends. Then I asked if they are only going to have fun with the girls why do they spend so much time trying to look their best? They all said they like to look good when they go out and didn't see anything wrong with that. I also asked if they looked good just in case someone saw them? They all said yeah. I then asked if they saw a guy that they thought was attractive would they go talk to him or would they wait for him to come to them? The ladies replied they would wait for him to come to her, or she would make him notice her, but wouldn't talk to him first.

I came to the conclusion that ladies see someone that they are interested in, but they won't talk to him, because he has to talk to the lady first. That doesn't make sense to me. If I'm somewhere and I see someone that I'm interested in, I'm going to say something to them. So I asked why they wouldn't say anything and why was it important to them that the guy speaks first, or that they guy notices the woman first? They all said, "We are women and if a man likes us he will come talk to us." So my final question was if he never said anything to them would they do what they had to do for him to notice them? They all said yeah and laughed. Women are planners and they play out all scenarios in their mind.

Let me explain how it works. The woman sees you, she tells her friend I want to meet him, later on she moves into your line of sight, she gave you a slick little eye to let you know that she noticed you too. That is all you needed to make your move on her, you needed to know that she may be interested. The one thing you didn't know was that you didn't have to say much to her at all, you wasted like five minutes trying to make conversation. You could have walked over and said "Let me have your number I will call you later," and you would have still got her number.

There's a big difference between men and women; women work together to get what they want while men go on every mission solo. For example you spot a chick at the bar and you tell your homeboy to look at her. Of course he told you to go get her, not paying attention to the factors around him. Meanwhile her best friend's girl was right in front of both of you the whole time. This is why I have to ask the questions who is gaming who?

Fellas have you ever left work and bumped into the same girl three out of the five days that you leave work? It's not a coincidence, but the plan of the female. Let me tell you a Story . . .

Back in 2000 I worked for the Sheriff department and noticed that we had a few dimes (pretty young ladies) in the academy. There was one young lady that I was feeling above any of the others. She was sassy and had an edge, I like my chicks to have a little hood in them. She was tall with long thick legs and had all the nice curves like Beyonce Knowles. She had no waist what so ever, that led you right up to her breast that didn't need a bra. Her face was caramel, with a smile that could light up any ones day. I wouldn't flirt with her because it was the police academy and I didn't know if I could get arrested for that, but I did look at her sexy body every chance I got. I did notice that throughout the academy she always ended up in my group. She was a hard young lady to figure out because if I said something funny she would never laugh, everyone else would laugh. I figured she must have a husband or boyfriend and that was why she wasn't interested in Kenny Mack. I would soon find out that she was interested in me. She was running her game on me the whole time.

We started working in the jail and out of nowhere she called my cell phone one day. I really didn't think anything of it, but I was wondering how the hell she got my number? Don't get me wrong I wasn't mad that she had it just surprised. She called me one day and talked to me only about work, but at the end of the conversations I slid in an invitation to hang out after work, and she accepted. She and I ended up having sex a few times, and then I started to ask her questions. I asked her why she was always in my group. She was honest enough to tell me that, she thought I was cute so she did what she had to do to be close to me. She told me that she really wanted me to come on to her, but I never did, so finally so got my number from one of the co-workers. If a woman wants you she will get you one way or another, even if you don't know that she's coming on to you.

Long story short she was gaming me the whole time when I thought I had made the first move in asking her to hang out with me. Women have that sneaky game that is not readily noticed by the natural eye. You can even take one of my ex-girls for example. She used to walk down my street in hopes that I would see her and take her to work. That worked too, because I have such a good heart. I saw her walking and since I had a car I would run her to work. I think that you almost have to anticipate that a chick is running game before you can find out if she is for real or if she is the new man.

I remember this one girl at work used to come to work wearing whatever she wanted, not doing her hair and probably sometimes not brushing her teeth, just joking. I originally worked downstairs so I never knew who she was. I had never seen her before I started working upstairs so I never saw when she was not dressed nice. People told me that she use to dress like a homeless person before I moved upstairs. When I moved up to the floor she started dressing cute she started doing her wig every morning and she was oh so helpful with my new job. Hell I didn't know what the hell to do anyway I was just out there faking it until I made it. She and I were cool. I looked at her as a friend and a person that was there to help, but the truth was that she really wanted me. I remember she texted me late one night to ask, "What is there to do tonight?" I told her that she could go to the club or go have drinks, but there wasn't much going on that Saturday. She sent me a text back asking me to meet her for drinks, I was cool with that. We ended up having a platonic night of conversation and drinks, but from the conversation I could tell she wanted more. I realized then that she had done all that dressing nice and helping me because she wanted me to notice her. It was all game! I remembered how she used to lean across my desk just so I could see her breast, and then she would try to cover them up after I had already looked. She had a boyfriend that cheated on her and she wanted to use me as the person to get back at him. That was who I was supposed to be. It's crazy how women move. They always want to be able to tell their boyfriend that another guy came onto them when in reality they were the ones steadily giving all the signs that they wanted him.

Then you have to look at the females that give you that direct game; straight forward this is what I want. They do it in such a smooth way that you forget that it may be a slut move. I remember this one chick who sent me a Facebook inbox message when I was standing right in front of her. She wrote in her message, "don't look at me like that, it turns me on". Now that is real straight forward, in that message she let me know that whenever I wanted to I could have her. She was beautiful too. She was a Hispanic girl with a body, she put you in the mindset of J-Lo, but she wasn't J-Lo she was more like hey hoe! I ignored the message because my girl was sitting around 10 feet away from this chick. The real sad thing is that she knew I had a girl. She wanted to see how far I would go. I wasn't about to join into that set up. I laughed and kept it moving, but she kept at me all the time. She would text and ask me if I was going to come and get it or if she could touch it. I have to admit that it was kind of a turn on. I don't know how many men can continue to say no to beautiful young lady throwing herself at you unless you are married. A female that knows what she wants is one of the sexiest things in the world. I guess you can say that it worked out, because when my girl left me I took the straight forward female up on her offer. I remember the first night I stopped by. We had sex, I got dressed, and left. She didn't talk to me for like a week. I really didn't care, but I guess she felt like I treated her like a whore. One day she told me that she had never had anyone have sex with her and leave so quickly; which probably was bullshit. I fell for the game, apologized and I told her I thought all she wanted was sex. That was easy to assume considering that she had given me head at work before we did anything at all. All she really wanted was someone to love, but she was just going about it the wrong way. The sad thing was that she was a very pretty young lady and did not have to be that way to get me to notice her. Instead she ran her game and got what she wanted. She sold me on the fact that we was going to have sex as soon as we saw each other and I was completely ok with first date sex.

You can question yourself for years about who met who or did I really come on to this chick or did she want me to come on to her. The flirt game is one of the biggest ways to come on to a chick, and one of the easiest to detect. What happens when a woman doesn't flirt back? What happens when a woman doesn't even seem like she is interested? That does not mean that she is not interested in you; it means that she wants you to try harder. Some women still have that old school mentality that the man should make the first move. You can tell this when you notice that she keeps showing up right in your face. It is not an accident; it is part of her game to get you to notice her.

Women figure that if you see them enough, sooner than later you will say something to them. As soon as you say anything they will start the flirt game. Women know how to give you just enough to let you know that they are interested. The sad thing is that as guys we are thinking the whole time that you came on to them, when the female gamed you to approach them. Who is gaming who? I have no idea, but I do know that women have way more game than us.

# Chapter 4

## Re-create Yourself

The thing about game is that if you have game you can detect someone running game. However if you are the person that has more game than the next person, that person will never notice that you are running game on them. For instance, a woman will recreate her image to attract the person she wants. Now, a man would not think anything of these changes. We figure that they are only changing their appearance, when actually she saw your last girlfriend and she is doing her best to be just like her. What all guys should do is let their side girlfriends meet their main girlfriends. This way she can see why she is the side chick rather than the main chick. I promise that this will lead to some of the best sex that you've ever had. The side chick will make love to you like she got something to prove. She will start giving you the best perks in the world, and you might start thinking of making her the main one. Once that side girlfriend has seen that main girlfriend, you might as well throw the jump ball up because the game has begun. She is going to try to do everything better than the next female. This is not because she really wants you, it's because she does not want to lose the game. You can start saying things just to get her to do things for you. You can say "you know my girl always shaves my butt hairs." Watch that side chick bring clippers over to your house the very next day; she might even bring some man Nair. She is going to want to win at all cost. The side chick will even start telling you that she loves you. She is going to re-create her self to be exactly what she thinks you want. The funny thing is that if you don't know what is going on, you will be fooled. The next thing you know you are leaving your main girl for this side chick when she isn't even close to meeting the standards of your main girl.

One of the courses I took was about the importance of having a good physical appearance. I surveyed a group of women and asked them if they were single would they go to the store in a housecoat and rollers. Most of them said no because you never know who you will run into. Women put a lot of time and preparation into their appearance so they can attract a man. If you find yourself dating someone at work or someone that has been around you for a while you will see that they will start wearing a lot of the outfits you like. Once you give them a compliment on their hair, jeans, shirt, shoes, or whatever they are going to keep a heavy dose of that coming at you. Sooner or later you will ask them out. They will continue to reinvent their selves until they look like the person you would date. That is all part of their game. There is no question that we would all like to look nice when we go out, but women look nice for the man that they want when they go out. If they want a hood dude they are going to wear the big earrings, a bunch of weave and an outfit that says I know how to drop down and get my eagle on. If they are looking for a business dude they are going to wear a nice fitting suit or dress, studs and very little makeup. That's another reason why women have way more game then men because they prepare their selves for everything that they want. If you happen to meet a young lady that claims to be real, you should ask to see some older pictures to see how she used to look. I promise you that it will not be anything like the way she looks now.

I remember this one chick I use to mess with, Jenny. When we first got together I thought that she was who she said she was. Eventually we fell out and I left her for another female. A few months later we meet up again and she was claiming that she was completely different than she used to be. Jenny tried her best to make me believe that she was the type of female that I was looking for. She flipped the game on me and had me believing that I had messed up when I let her go. Jenny was fine and she could have had any guy she wanted. The mask that she put on made me feel so special. Jenny didn't want to lose me so she did what she had to do to get me back. It didn't sit well with Jenny that I had left her, especially since she had never experienced someone not wanting her. So she reinvented herself into the person that she noticed that I liked. I have to admit I did start back messing with Jenny; I just didn't let my other female go.

Jenny had me messed up for a while. I was supposed to be trying to make my relationship work at home, and here she was with payback on her mind. I fell right into it because we had been in love at one point and I thought it was all the same. I don't know if Jenny really cared for me, what I can tell you is that she cared enough to want to get her revenge on my girl, and I just let it happen. See women run game in many ways. When are we really ready for their game? When do you know if it is real or fake?

I remember this one young lady that I was with who knew that I had recently gotten my heart broken. Maria tried to do whatever she could to make me forget my girl. Maria was beautiful and had no reason in the world to act like she acted, but I wasn't about to stop her when I was getting everything I wanted. The average guy may have felt like he hit the jackpot with Maria. Maria would have sex anywhere, go down on me anywhere, and she always wanted to have sex. Maria always took care of me too. She bought me everything, food, Ipod's, and she would cook for me. Maria was actually a good catch. She was Hispanic with a black girl booty; you have to love them when they look like that. She was just damaged goods and was in the process of re inventing herself to fit the person she thought I wanted. I admit getting head in the waffle house parking lot while the people inside watched was a hell of an adventure; even the women in the waffle house gave me dap for pulling that off. It made me question the young lady's integrity. Maria did whatever I asked her to do to make me want to stay with her. She really wanted me to forget my last relationship and move on with her. I told her that I still loved my last girl and Maria was like, "it's ok, you will love me too." Her game was transparent, but a lot of fellows would not recognize that she was even running game. She didn't really care for me like that she had an attraction of me, but not to the point where she seemed obsessed to please me. Maria saw me for who I was and wanted to put her stamp on me. She thought I was a good catch because I am smart, handsome, had a good job and my sex game was good. All of the strange places that we had sex were great, but the truth was I wasn't ready to move on to another relationship, I was just trying to have fun. Plus, once again, I was enjoying the perks, hell a home cooked meal every night, sex every night, in the morning, and sometimes just riding down the street. Who could beat that?

Guys you have to watch out for women with an agenda. She wanted a man in her life at all cost. Maria did not care who it was, I was just someone that she liked, and she thought her actions would make me love her, but sex has never made me love anyone. The fact that I didn't fall for her game led to Maria doing and saying a lot of things that weren't true which eventually led to my ex-girl being hurt.

At one point I truly believed that Maria was a good girl. I later realized that she was just scared and felt like she needed to run some kind of game to get me to like her. If I would have been in a different place in my life I may have fell victim to the bull she was shoveling. She had recreated herself to be a wild chick that was down for whatever because I told her that I liked hood chicks with class.

The change in a woman can either be a subtle change or a big one. Take independent females that are used to doing for their selves. Once they get a man that doesn't want them to work, and would like for them to stay at home you'd best believe that if that woman wants that man she will do what ever he asks her to do to make him happy. Even though that's not what's going to make her happy she will play the game to keep the man. Women will recreate their selves to please their man at all cost; you ask how is that game? That is just like when a man makes himself seem more important than he really is to get a female to like him. He may tell you that he runs the company he works for when all he does is answer the phones, or run the cleaning supply closet. Women have the option of doing the same thing. They can make a man think this is who they really are when they are not. Sometimes being yourself is the hardest thing to do in life, but if someone doesn't love you for who you are you shouldn't want them to love you anyway.

# Chapter 5

# "True Lies"

Women who cheat rarely have to lie. Women plan their cheating out 100%, while men just move with the wind and create the cover story later. Let's take a woman who lives in one city and her man lives in another. She is never going to spend the night at the guy's house she is cheating with; the guy will always come to hers. The reason they do it like that is so when her boyfriend calls to ask questions she can answer them truthfully. There's always less to explain when you're in your own home. Plus men feel like no one can put it down like them, but sex is not the reason women cheat. Women don't take chances. If they know you don't want them to talk to a guy on the phone they will not talk to him on the phone. Men always ask the wrong question, "you still talking to him on the phone?" and the true answer is no. She doesn't talk to him on the phone; she communicates with him through emails and text messages, but she never talks to him on the phone. Females will never save an email; they delete them as soon as they read it. You will never be able to go into a females email and find out that she is cheating on you unless you watch her email all day and night. Men get caught because they never think their girl suspects that they are cheating. Word to the wise, women always suspect something. If you are going to cheat, which I don't recommend, you should move like she is already on to you. That is how women move and that is how women can have extra boyfriends for years and their real boyfriend never know. One of the females I was with for over ten years never stopped talking to her previous boyfriend. I was played hard because I never asked the right questions. Really, I didn't ask any questions because I never thought she would cheat on me. But I learned from that, and took that lesson into my next relationships. Hopefully you all will learn from this too and take this to your next relationships.

Let me take this one girl I was messing with, we will call her Hope. Her boyfriend lived in DC. Hope texted me late one night to ask if had I heard that song *I Won't Tell*. I found the song and listened to it. Now would you believe that when I listened to the song it was a cheating song? I figured she was sexy, she wanted me, so why not. The song was her way of telling me that she wanted me, without her actually saying "I want you Mack." Hope and I hooked up later that week, and of course it was first night sex because we both knew that was all we wanted. I started going over a little more and she would cook for me and I would spend nights there. Her boyfriend would call every night and I would lay right beside her in her bed and listen to her tell this guy true lies. He would ask "where you at?" She would say "at home." He would say "what are you doing." She would say "laying down watching T.V." None of which were lies, that was what she was really doing at the time he asked.

The key is to make women either lie to you, or be honest. Men have to become the master of getting the lie. If you are away from home, ask your girl, "who are you watching TV with?" That is going to force her to lie or come clean. But keep in mind that women have game and won't give up that easy. The smart ones are going to answer your question with a question; "what you mean who am I watching TV with?" Then they will say, "I can't believe you would ask me a question like that, you don't trust me do you"? Now they have you answering questions and they haven't lied or answered the question you put right in front of them. The next thing you know, you're sitting there thinking that you've messed up. They have you too scared to even follow up with the questions and get a direct answer, because the sad thing is that you really trust them. You must make your questions direct and get the answers you want from them, because if you don't they will confuse you. Their ultimate goal is to always say that they have never lied to you. After they flip the situation and make it seem like you were in the wrong for even asking them any questions, they pretend that they are mad that you would even think such a thing. What you were feeling was true; they were indeed at home with someone else. They were lying in the bed with someone else. But they have flipped the situation around so bad they have you apologizing to them, telling them you were just playing or you were just asking. So the whole point was to start a fight to get off the phone with you quick. Now they have a reason to get off the phone with you quickly and get back to their penis in the bed beside them, while you go to bed feeling bad. That's called flipping it! They took the spotlight off them and put it on you. Now you believe her. They still have not lied. Then they say things to make you feel better about yourself like, "Why would I want anyone else when I have you?" And you are eating those words up, but remove your ego for a second and realize that most men can do exactly what you do. Realize she didn't say she didn't want anyone but you, she said, "Why would I want anyone else when I have you?" There are a lot of answers to that question if you look deeper, and you start looking deep enough you would be on the next flight to your girl's house right then.

My grandmother used to say "a lie don't care who tell it". She didn't say that, I really don't know my grandmother like that, but I know old people say it, so it must be right. The way you ask a question and the answer that you get is the real lie, remember truth can be a lie. Truth is what ever you want it to be. I had a female once tell me, and she was completely serious, "I don't care if someone saw me doing it, if I say it wasn't me, it wasn't me." It is up to the listener to determine if he wants to believe the person that told him that she was doing something or his girl. He probably trusts his girl so he will choose to believe her. One female told me that she never answered questions, she said that she did it so much that her boyfriend learned how to ask the right questions. He could ask her where did you go last night, and she would turn right around and ask him where he went. His answer to her would always start a fight about the things that he did, and she would not have to talk about what she did. That's a person with game. It was so funny because I would do the same thing to my first girl. Some of you fellas are reading this right now, and replaying fights with your significant other in your head, and realize that you just got played. When your girl starts those random fights I promise on everything they are in no way shape or form mad at you. They know if you are able to get the truth out of them, your ass will be mad. True lies, they haven't lied they just never answered the questions.

It's all Game; males did it for years now women are the masters. Men are just peasants to their mental games. True lies, real lies, and little white lies all add up to game.

# Chapter 6

## "Check the Stats"

Women have a strange way of seeming very honest when the reality is they are far from that. When you feel like you are falling for a young lady try and remember how you met her. That was always my problem; always giving people the benefit of doubt. When fellas get serious with someone they start asking the real questions like, how many people has she been with, how many real relationships has she been in. I know you all remember asking a lady how many people she's been with and response was that she could count all the people she's been with on one hand. She didn't really lie because she can actually use one hand to count all of the people that she had been in a serious relationship with. The female will make it sound so believable by saying something like, "I just can't do it to people like that, I have to know you or feel something for you to have sex." Then you ask her what's so different about you because she had sex with you on the first night? That's when she boosts your ego by saying, "I know, I normally don't do that, but it was just something about you, you are just so sexy and I already liked you so much." Come on fellas, check the stats. That is the exact same thing she said to the last man she had sex with on the first night.

I have had a lot of first night females and all of them say the same thing. That they normally don't do stuff like that, or they blame their last man and call it a phase. Now I would have to say those are things that groupies say. I know that most men don't fall for the bull that they are shoveling, but women seem so honest that you almost have to give them the benefit of the doubt. Women know that men have huge egos and that is why they play on them so hard. They tell you everything you want to hear, they yell you're the best; they say you are the sexiest person in the world. I'm so confused because I know that women kick bull, but I had sex with both of my true loves on the first night that we kicked it. I know, I know, I sound like a hypocrite telling you all not to fall for it when I did not once but twice. Hey, who is better to tell you about it than someone who has been through it? It's funny, because they were both the best, mentally and sexually I ever had. They kicked it to me hard; telling me they loved me after a few months. I told them too because I really felt that I loved them. I have no idea if it was only game, but in the end both of them did the same thing, cheat on me. I always wondered how a person could cheat on the best they've ever had? Then again, I cheated on them too. Maybe that is why I gave both the benefit of doubt, but there isn't any benefit of doubt when you're dealing with game. I look back on both relationships and laugh because both of them introduced me to game. They showed me the importance of checking the stats on women before chilling with them and catching feelings.

They each used a different type of game on me. My first love really loved me and wanted me to love her back. She tried to make herself honest by being really careful with what she told me. My second love only wanted me to think she loved me. She always seemed honest as well, but her goal was only to make the next man jealous. I was hit with all kind of red flags that should have told me not to love them, but I was blinded by love.

I remember when my first love and I dated we had a conversation about all the people we had been with. We'll call her "Kalee". Kalee went the extra mile and named all of the people that she had been with. I was thinking damn she didn't have to do that, I was just asking how many. She gave me more than I asked for so it seemed like she was being really honest. The truth was that she was only telling me just enough. By giving names, telling me when she did it, and all that extra stuff, she eliminated a lot of follow up questions. I was content with the answer she gave me because it seemed so truthful. It is funny how karma works because not even a week later that conversation caught up with her. I came home from school to surprise her. When I got to her house she was on the porch with another dude, braiding his hair. The surprise was on me. I asked her if she wanted to get up and she said she did after she finished his hair. Hell, it was already like 9 o'clock at night. So I said ok and bounced. I remembered all of the names of the dudes she had sex with and he wasn't one of them. The next day Kalee called me to let me know that nothing happened. She said that she had promised that she would braid his hair and she hated breaking promises. That was just more game. It was just nice way of telling me that she wanted to be with him rather than me. I thought, "I'm your boyfriend forget a promise, what about me?" But back to the story, I was straight because that night I did what I have always done; I found someone that would chill with me. Kalee called me at school later that week crying, like a big baby. She told me that the guy whose hair she was braiding called her and told her that he had an STD. She was crying so bad that my sister actually had to finish the conversation. To make a long story short we went and got check out and neither one of us had it, Thank God. I had been fooled. She had omitted his name because she was still messing with him. She wanted to make sure that if I ever saw him I wouldn't think anything of them being around one another. That was my first little taste of some of that honest game. A woman's game is planned out. They move like a chess game, about three steps ahead. Kalee wanted to be able to be with both of us, so it was premeditated to omit the name of the other guy she was sleeping with. That is why you have to check the stats because what you are told is probably not completely true. If it seems like they are being really honest, they are, everything they are saying is true, and everything they are not saying you will never know, unless karma intervenes.

I should have put two and two together and known that a woman was not going to tell me everything anyway. I should have focused on the fact that I had sex with her on the first night when I didn't even know her phone number. Now those are the stats that I should have really checked out. The main thing that you have to remember is that a woman knows how much a man can take. They know what they should tell and what they shouldn't. To keep their man they will omit a lot of things that they feel he will not be able to handle.

# Chapter 7

## "Did you really say that?"

I know I talk a lot about what I have a seen and what I perceive is game by women, and I know a lot of my fellas out there normally peep game from women. The truth is that most of the time you don't know for sure if a woman is running game, but you know what game sounds like. Women are the masters of saying what you need to hear to make you secure, even when they are completely in the wrong. If you ever catch your female cheating, and you know you have her completely busted, she is going to find out how much you know before she comes clean. You have to look out and listen hard to make sure you are hearing everything completely.

I remember I was kicking it with this female, and I was sort of living at her crib. One day Pam told me that she was going to stay at her mom's house that night, and before she got off the phone she told me that she loved me. It was crazy because we never said I love you before we got off the phone. So I knew it was some B S. I blame myself because I should have known that she wasn't any good. For starters I had sex with her on the first night, she had a boyfriend and she approached me for sex. I had fell into the zone where I kind of liked her, hell I spent almost every night at her house. She did so much for me, so of course I had some kind of feeling for her. In my heart I knew she was lying and trying to run game, so I had to ask myself, why did she really say I love you? So I did what most men would do; I stopped by her house that night and saw that she was right at home. I called her and of course she did not answer. Then I called her house phone and she didn't answer, so I sent her a text asking where she was? She texted me back with the classic line, "what you mean where am I at?" So I just told her, "I know that you are at home, I don't know who you are there with, but I know that you are there." Then her story changed, "yeah I'm home I just felt like being alone for the night." It was funny because even though she knew she was caught, she still tried to cover it up. I was laughing so hard at her still trying to lie. The story changed but the lies stayed the same. She was at home but she was having sex with another dude, yet she told me that she loved me when we got off the phone. The fact was that she had a boyfriend, who she was cheating on me with, and another dude who she was using to cheat on both of us. That's how they try and run game, they will tell you something that you want to hear so they can do what ever they want.

My second true love was really good for that. She would say whatever she thought that I wanted to hear to make things up with me. She would go the extra mile and do what ever I wanted; sometimes things I would not even ask for, but I would not complain about getting it. There were plenty of nights that she came right over to my house because I was mad at her just to have sex with me. That was her game; she knew what I liked and what would make me still feel the same about her. I fell for it all the time. That is what females do, they feel their man out and know what it takes to make him forget or not question something that is kind of suspect.

I remember one time my second true love and I had started really kicking it and she told me that she was on the way home. I could hear the echo of the bathroom in the background so I knew she was still at her baby daddy's house. When we were getting off the phone she told me that she loved and missed me and wished she could come see me that night. She actually could have come to see me that night, but she wanted to be somewhere else. I knew she was lying by the tone of her voice and how quickly she tried to get off the phone with me. I ran a little game to get her to be honest with me. About an hour later I texted her and asked her where she was. Of course she hit me with "what you mean where I'm at? I already told you." She didn't know that I knew she was lying. I lied to her and told her that I had driven by her house and her car wasn't there, when the truth was that I was at home. The way she answered my questions led me to play the card that was going to force her to be honest. I didn't want her trying to make our relationship seem like it was something that it wasn't. She finally told the truth, well it probably wasn't the whole truth, and said that she stayed over there so they could talk. Then she did the ego boost thing and said that the conversation was all about how she felt about me. If all they were doing was talking then why was it so hard to be honest? I told her that I wasn't messing with her on that level anymore. I played the sympathy card and told her how hurt I was. The sad thing was that I had really started to like her at that point. The next day she came to my house and did it to me really good. The whole time we were having sex she was telling me that it was mine and she wasn't going anywhere. I have to admit that she had me fooled because I started to believe that she only went over there to talk. From that point on I didn't trust her any more, so I really should have called it quits and just kept her around for sex. The more time we spent together the more I forgot about everything else and my heart took the lead. What I should have been asking was did you really say that? Did you really say that it was mine, when you gave it away the day before; did you really say you loved me and missed me and wish you could see me when you are at another dudes house? They were just words with very little meaning, but the way she said it made me assess value to her words, when I should have taken them for what they were worth; nothing at all.

Sometimes you ask what they really meant when they said that or when she did what she had to do to make you happy. Most of the time it is game, like home girl that told me that she loved me so I would think everything was on the up and up, when she was trying to get some different penis. It's a game in words and in their actions. I used to have a chick that would give me head all the time, every time I saw her, we didn't even have sex; she would just give me head and send me on my way. Now you tell me what guy would not want to keep a chick like that on your team. I was stupid I should have cut her off after like the fifteenth time but it was just what the doctor ordered most nights. She knew that I loved her head and that was her game to keep me around, hell I seen that physiatrist (head doctor) for about three years. I had girlfriends that she knew about, hell some of them were her friends. She just played the cool roll like she didn't care and that she was going to get what she wanted anyway. I let her get what she wanted too, because she was giving me what I wanted. It was all game though, that was her way of trying to make me like her. It's funny she and I never went out unless she was buying me drinks or something. She used to tell me that she loved me all the time. I kept her around to long, and that is when things started going crazy and I found out that she was crazy too. I started feeling bad that I didn't love her back and I would still go and chill with her, I would still go and have sex with her, just because I felt that she really loved me. The truth was she didn't love me she just wanted to win, she wanted to keep me around long enough so that I would love her too. I almost fell for the game, but I knew she was only looking for a man and was willing to do or say anything to make me stay.

That is the power of what women say and do, the statements that really makes you laugh are the ones that you listen to and don't want to add the true value to it. Every chick that I had sex with on the first night all said the same thing "I normally don't do stuff like this." Come on man; that is that bull. My issue has always been I kept them around too long. My first love was a first nighter and my second love was a first nighter. You think that I would have learned my lesson by now, you'd think that I would somehow figure out that if you light a match you are going to feel the flame. I kept both of them around long enough that I fell in love. When I really should have been asking, "Did you really just say that?"

I remember my second love, the first night we went out we had sex, she gave me head and everything. The next day we are talking and the first thing she said was "I did not plan to have sex with you, we were only supposed to have had drinks and that's it!" She also said, "I can't believe that I gave you head I don't even do that!" Then why did you do it to me? I do have to admit that I am a different dude from most guys, so anytime someone says they want to have drinks, we would come to my house. I have drinks at my house and a bed too. That is why my second love said that she did not expect to be at my house having drinks. I should have known better than to keep kicking it with her, but for me it wasn't about being in a relationship with her it was about the sex. Sometimes even when you only make the situation only about the sex it's hard to stop what you feel for someone. Then you add all the game into what you may be feeling and their words with no real value start having meaning. They tell you that they love you, you are the best that they've ever had, they never expected to feel this way about you, and all the things that you want to hear but don't want to believe you are starting to fall for. A woman's game is on a level that most men can't match. Fellas play games for the night, women play games for life.

I have to laugh now when I hear females say things like that because I know that they want you to respect them just a little bit. I have to admit, and I know all my fellas will agree, that if you continue to have sex with a woman after the first night sex, you are going to over look the fact that she let you hit it on the first night. It's just in a man's nature to continue having sex with her. In a perfect world you would just hit it that one time and move on, but there are other factors that go into the longevity of those relationships. If she is fine, there is no way that you are not going to hit it again, if it was good, and don't let her be nasty, you going to wonder how nasty can she really get. Women know this, so they use sex as a weapon that keeps you coming back. Then they do things like offer to take you out. You go out and have good conversation, then you start to like her, and you're thinking back to the first night and saying maybe she really doesn't usually do things like that on the first night. That's how they get you, they make you believe that you are different that was the only reason you were able to get it on the first night. The truth is that you are different and that is why you got it on the first night. The difference was that she liked you, the guys that don't get it on the first night she didn't like. I'm not saying that you are the only person that she ever liked on the first night. That is why you have to roll with it, and realize that what they are really saying is that if they didn't like you they wouldn't have had sex with you. They are not saying that they have never done anything like that, notice they said "I *normally* don't do things like this."

The thing that is really funny that women say and they use it as the deal sealer. They tell you that you are their best. Now be honest with yourself, usually the best sex that a woman has is with the person that she loves. That's not saying that you can't be bigger than him or that you can't make her reach her peak a little bit more than he does, but you are not him. The reason why a woman will tell you that you are her best is because she knows that will play into the male ego. Once you think that you are the best you will also think that she is never going to want anyone else. This is not true, women are similar to men in the way that if they see something that they like and it is obtainable then they go for it. Telling you that you are the best is only to put your mind at ease. The truth is that those are only words and words are usually bull. Actions are what tell the true story of who you are and what you are about. The reason why it's so funny to me is because probably 95% of the women that I have been with told me that I was their best. All of them only told me that so I would stay. I admit having that in the back of my mind did provide me with the insurance that they wouldn't go anywhere. My second love told me that I was her best, yet and still she would still have sex with her baby's daddy all the time. I may have been her best, but she loved him and I couldn't compete with that. She told me what I wanted to hear so I would not feel threaten by him. I wasn't threatened sexually by him, but I did know that he had her heart. She told me all the time that she wasn't in love with him and that she loved me, and that I was who and what she wanted. I should have been asking "did you just say that?" Telling me that I was her best led me to believe that she would not go anywhere. The way I use to put it down on her, and how she would react to me really made me think that it was true. I should have known that it was just what I wanted to hear, and she knew that so she would tell me all the time.

It's all game, how deep will you fall into the words of a female, hell I was in love twice overlooking the obvious. Don't fall victim to what they say or what they do, a woman that will give you head wherever, and she is not your wife, is a good female to keep on your team but that should be as far as it goes. A woman that lets you hit on the first night, then tell you that she doesn't normally do things like that. Those words are only telling you that she likes you. You have to remember that they are just words that really make you think, make you consider, maybe she doesn't. All you need to consider is that she did it to you, so you best believe that you are not the first and you will not be the last.

Women love to say things that will throw you off, make you not consider what they are really doing. They may tell you I love you, I miss you, I wish that you were here, and the favorite thing for them to say is I wish I didn't have to go tonight, but I promised my friend. When they say things like that they are cheating on you. Just remember to ask yourself, did you say that?

# Chapter 8

## "Women are the Best Cheaters"

I have to admit that men are sloppy cheaters. I've learned how to cheat and get away with it from being in a relationship with the number one crime detective ever. She could find out anything and I never knew how she was so insightful. During the time we dated and I probably cheated on her about 100 times and she caught me 50 of them. During the end of our relationship she couldn't catch me anymore, because she had taught me what not to do so well. I also learned from her that you can cheat for years and never get caught. In my relationships after her, I cheated all the time and would never get caught. I'm as good as a woman when it comes to cheating. I learned from sitting right beside women as they talk to their boyfriends and from listening to my only true loves talk, I became the best male cheater ever. I'm not sure if that is something that I should brag about. That is why I'm completely faithful now. Why are you smiling while you are reading this like you don't believe me?

Men think that women cheat because they know you are cheating, or because you're not good enough for them. Women cheat because they feel like they are missing something. When a woman cheats she is going to have everything in order, everything already planned out. She will also make sure that it is a solo mission so she won't have to include anyone else in her lie. That is the best way to move, the less people that know the better off you are. If you ever think that you're woman is cheating, you almost have to believe that she is telling you the truth, because there is no one to verify her story. If you start to question her, she will pull out the trust card and say, "so you don't trust me" and what you should say is, "Hell no," but instead you apologize for even questioning her. That is part of their game; they make you think that they are the most honest person in the world when the truth is that they are just one of the most clever people in the world. The insight, the planning, and the lack of a cover up story is the best way to cheat. Women live by, the less is more concept. When they cheat they may not even tell you that they are going anywhere. When you get home and they are not there you probably won't even think anything. They will come home with a few things from the store and you naturally assume that they were at the store. You may not even ask where they were because less is more, the less they have to say the better off they are with getting away with it.

Women play the game to the fullest, and they plant seeds that make it easier for them to cheat. Fellas you all have had women that never keep their phone on them. There is a reason why they don't keep their phone near them. They sometimes will take hours to respond to you. It's game. By establishing that they never have their phone on them from the very first time you call them it makes it easier for you to believe that they just didn't have their phone on them when you tried to call them. It's all premeditated, they know a day is going to come when they are at their other boyfriend's house and cannot answer their phone. They will always be able to say, "I just saw you called me, you know I don't keep my phone on me." That's that real game, write it down, rip the page out, do something! Fellas we need to know this stuff. You see them all the time and you know they keep their phone in their car, they keep their phone in the kitchen, or they just conveniently forget to take it out their purse every time they come home. That is why in your heart you have to believe that they did not have their phone and that they just saw your missed call. See that's where men mess up we keep our phone so close to us, every time your girl call you answer. When you don't answer your phone you have to come up with an excuse. Now because you had to make up an excuse why you didn't answer your phone now you have to remember that lie for the next time she ask you. You didn't follow the code of less is more, now you have added more to the story and you run a greater risk of being caught.

My two true loves use to keep their cell phones on vibrate all the time. My first love would turn her phone completely off every time she came home. The reason why they kept their phone on vibrate and put away was so I would never hear their phones ring. The reason that my first love gave me for turning her phone off was because anyone that needed to contact her could call her on the house phone. You could get grand and say, "turn your phone back on when you come home with me." But how stupid would you look and sound saying that? I would not say anything at all, and let them have their way. My first love really taught me about premeditated cheating; she was really good. I would have never known that she was cheating on me if my friend didn't blow up her spot at work. For me that was my first lesson learned in how to cheat. She set boundaries for her boyfriend, he knew never to call her, she would call him, he knew that it was only sex, and he knew never to even come around her at work. When I found out that my first love was cheating on me, she was already finished messing with the dude. Now you can't tell me that she wasn't an expert cheater. It is funny being around her now that we are not together, because she has ringtones on her phone for everyone that calls. Her phone is always on, and turned all the way up, but that's because I'm not her man. When I was her man she supposedly hated ringtones and didn't like to be bothered at home so she kept her cell phone off. It was all just a game just a safety net, that would keep her from ever getting caught.

My second love was the same way, but by the time I was with her I was prepared for that game. I would just laugh when she and I would be making love and her phone would be vibrating in her purse. I loved how once we were finished she would go through all her messages and show me the one from her friend girls, like that was the only time her phone went off. It was funny as heck, because that's what I use to do, I would read and erase any messages or calls I had from females and say some stupid shit like "my homeboy always texting me late, sending me some forward look at this baby." That would always keep the peace. Women know that number one, the man is going to feel some kind of way if they just act like their phone didn't go off and number two if you don't show some proof that it was nothing you will be in trouble. My second love knew that all too well, she is the female me, I promise you she has more game then a little bit. I would sometime call her on her BS but most of the time I just took it in stride and would point it out to her later.

I remember one young lady I was messing with had a boyfriend, but loved to have sex with me. Once I was going out of town on a company trip and she went out of town on that same fake company trip, at least that is what she told her boyfriend. Hell she even made up her own paper work and left it lying around her house so he could read it. She planned it out perfect and made sure that she did not have to include anyone else in her lie. Plus we were out of town so no one had to see us. Her boyfriend never asked any questions. Now that is what you call being an expert cheater. That is why women can get away with it, because you better believe the person that they are cheating with is going to know that they have a boyfriend that is more important then them. If their boyfriend happens to call while they are with the other guy they can answer the phone and talk to him as long as he wants. This removes all doubt in their real boyfriends mind that they are even doing anything wrong. I sat there plenty of times and just let them talk to their boyfriend while I watched T.V. I would just listen to those women tell their man that they loved them, that they missed them, everything he wanted to hear. As soon as they would hang up the phone they were right back taking my pants off. See that's were men mess up, we try and lie to the next girl and tell her that you are single that you are not messing with any one, when the truth is so much easier to manage. Then when your main girl calls you can't answer because your mistress doesn't know, she thinks and assumes that you all are working towards a relationship. I learned to be honest with females, I would tell them that I have a wife and a girlfriend so if we do anything it is only going to be sexual. Try it fellas the truth is so much easier.

I had a female tell me how she cheated on her boyfriend at the beach while he was there. Tell me that she isn't the illest (The best). She bought a pre paid phone, and gave that number to the other dude that she wanted to see, and her boyfriend knew nothing about the second phone. The other guy had no idea that she was even there with her boyfriend. She was able to get up with both of them most days that she was down there, without even saying anything. She would never tell either one of them where she was going she would just go. She told me that she soon found out that it wasn't even worth cheating on her man, because the other guy was so weak in bed. The story was one of the realest I had ever heard. I do have to admit that she was the female with the most game out of all the females that I have ever messed with or been with. The sad thing is she is the female version of me. I told her that all the time, the things that she had done sounded so much like me. The difference was that I used to get caught, and she never did.

Women are by far better cheaters than men, so by far they have way more game then us. Men fall victim into trying to always be there for a women. Men try to answer the phone every time their girl calls, men try to come home right after work so their girl won't expect anything. Women don't mind telling you that they just got your message an hour after you sent it. They don't mind showing up a few hours later than they normally do. That's all in the set up, women already know that the day is going to come when they need to use that excuse, I just got your message, or you know it always take me a long time in the store after work. Women set rules with there men on the side, so that there will not be any confusion about what that side dudes position is. Women keep nothing, no emails, text messages, phone call history, everything is erased right when they receive it. You are never going to be able to find your girl's Facebook page up and find a message from her boyfriend, they are too good for that. To catch a women cheating you have to pray to the relationship Gods, which means the Lord, and ask him to show you what you need to see. Just don't be like me and fall in love with the wrong females.

# Chapter 9

## "Payback or Playback"

The one thing that any man doesn't want to happen is to get caught cheating on his girl. Once you get caught, she is going to take advantage of that and have sex with all the dudes that she had turned down. It's like taking over the main street in a town and turning all the lights green. Your girl will probably break up with you and tell you that it is over. When she really doesn't want to break up with you, she only wants you to pay for what you did to her. She is going to keep you close, still invite you to her house and still let you have sex with her. You are going to feel like she has forgiving you and that you all are moving forward. What she is really doing is, waiting until you get real comfortable, then you are going to call her one night and you won't get an answer. Trust and believe that she is going to let you catch her or she is going to flat out tell you that she cheated on you. The only reason she tells you is that she wants to see your reaction, plus payback is a must. The fact is the person that she chooses to cheat on you with is the person that she already wanted to cheat with anyway. So what you did was open the door for what she wanted to do anyway. The goal now is to make it seem like it is your fault that she even did such a thing. Tank messed it up for all of us guys, making that damn song *Maybe I Deserve*, because that's what gave women the idea that it was ok. I promise you after she tells you that she has been with someone else the next time you see her she will be playing Tank *Maybe I Deserve*. Then you are standing there listening to the song saying maybe I did deserve for her to cheat on me.

I remember I made a mistake by cheating on my first girlfriend and telling her. She did everything that she could to let me know that she was sleeping with someone else. I have to admit it did make me feel some kind of way, but it was really too early in my life for me to feel the impact. I wasn't that mad at her for doing it, but it did make me look at her in a different way. My first girlfriend cared for me a lot and wanted me to care for her. She did what she did because she wanted me to feel the same pain that she felt. I remember when she told me. Jennifer came to me and said I have something to tell you and I don't want you to be mad. I had a feeling what Jennifer was going to tell me, in my heart I wanted to know, but then I didn't want to know. Jennifer came right out and said that she had sex with her old boyfriend. I felt that was crazy, because that is the guy that she was with right before me, and she left him for me. It played with my mind and she knew that. She was sending me a message that she could have anyone she wanted, and if I didn't treat her right, someone else would. Jennifer had told me all about how he was trying to get back with her while she and I were together. Jennifer knew that having sex with him would mess with me a lot more than having sex with a random dude. That was her game; she wanted me to feel like I needed to be with her so that she couldn't be with him. The truth was she didn't want to be with him, because she was at my house about to have sex with me again. When I was young I bottled my emotions so I just shook it off like it didn't matter at all.

I played it really cool and had sex with her and went on my way. It did hurt me that she would do such a thing to me, even though I cheated first and we were broke up when she did what she did. None of that was the point, the point was that she was mine, she still acted like mine, she still was there for me like she was my girl. So it really confused me why she would mess with her old boy friend. Now that I am older I see the mind games that women play, and when I think back to situations like that I realize that it was just a game.

That is the cost that you pay as a man when you cheat on your girl. I know you all remember the movie The Best Man. That was the ultimate, the one person that she cheated with hurt him worse than all the girls he cheated with combined. That's how women move they don't just go for revenge; they are going to take your heart and everything else. They are hoping that you realize that you love them more than some bullshit sex, and they are going to instill in your head that they can be with someone else besides you. That is when the man starts to playback everything that he has done to the female and starts to hear Tank playing in his head again.

I cheated on my first love all the time because I was an athlete, I was on the road all the time and women loved me. I could walk up to them and tell them that I was only in town for that night and they were trying to find a way to see me. I always thought about my girl though, but I was like what she doesn't know will not hurt her. When my first love and I dated, our relationship was the best and the worst. When we were together it was like we were meant to be. When we were apart both of us did our own thing. I remember I tried to come clean with her and tell her about all the cheating that had went on in our relationship. Why did I ever do that? Come to find out she knew about a lot of it. I had finished school and I was done playing and I was ready to marry her. I had waited just a little bit too long because she was ready to have fun. My first love told me that she did not want to get married right then, but she kept me around. She continued to have sex with me, she continued to go out with me and we would hang out sometimes. So I was thinking that I was making progress with her, and that maybe she would come around and marry me. But that was not what she was looking for; she was looking for revenge. I remember she and I had made plans to go out one night to the movies, she came straight to my house with hickies on her neck. I looked at her and said, "What is that on your neck?" She just smiled and said, "I think I got bit by something." At that point I was mad as all you know what, but we still ended up going out to the movies. While we were sitting in the movies, I saw more bug bites. I got up and walked out of the movies. She called me later on that night trying to explain and told me that it was a game they were playing and she didn't even know they were there. I laughed so hard and then we got off the phone, here is where it really gets stupid, she called me back and told me the truth out of the blue, that she was messing with this other dude. This is the same dude that she was claiming was her friend. Then she told me that she thinks that he was still on the phone when she called me. My first love wanted me to lie to him and say that she and I weren't having sex anymore. Now I can't tell you how bad that hurt, this was the girl that I loved asking me to cover for her for another dude. I hung up the phone on her, then I thought about it and I called her back and I said that I would do it, but I told her that she better not ever call me again. It turned out that he wasn't on the phone and he didn't hear our conversation, so I did not have to cover for her. My first love planned that out perfect. She set me up so good and that payback hurt me way more then any little thing I could have ever told her. That was her plan. She knew that she didn't want me anymore, but she kept me just close enough to really hurt me. All I could think was that she never loved me, because how could you really ask the person that you love to cover for you, for another dude. That's why if you cheat on your girl and she never finds out, thank your lucky stars. Don't go and grow a conscience, the pain that female gives you will be much worst in the end. My first love had no intentions of getting back with me; she only wanted to hurt me.

That is how females move, that's why I have to give it up to them and say they have way more game then us fellas. That's why you have to ask, are you really going to be able to playback your relations after you cheat? The answer to that is no because the only thing that you are going to playback is how nasty their payback felt. You may go on for months thinking that you and your girl are back straight and that everything that happened is really in the past. The reality is that everything that happened is still on the front of their minds and in the end you are going to wish you had never cheated.

# Chapter 10

## "My Friend Girls or Friendly Games"

Over my many years of being in and out of relationships I did have three friend girls. Two of them stem from high school and one, well I met her when I was five and from that point on I had a small crush on her. She by far was the hardest to stay away from sexually. I remember calling her house in the fourth grade and her father calling my father back and telling him that his little girl was not allowed to accept calls from boys. It's funny that I was trying to talk to females then. The age old questions is can a male be friends with a female, and can a female be friends with a male? Truth be told yes and no, because if both of you are attractive somebody is going to want to feel somebody's butt. The sad thing is once that friendship goes down that road of sexual contact it's hard to be friends again. But anyway, how do I explain how women have more game then men? Each and every one of my friend girls came on to me, but the sad thing is that I somewhat knew what they were doing I just blocked it out like it wasn't even happening.

Let's start with one of my friend girls from high school lets call her Natalie. Natalie was a very cool chick; everyone loved her. She was funny, sexy, and crazy. Natalie and I used to talk on the phone, we would hang out and go places but we never tried each other, at least I thought we never tried each other sexually.

Natalie had a boyfriend, and I had a girlfriend, somewhat, but not really. What I didn't pick up on from Natalie was the signs that she wanted me to be her boyfriend. Natalie would say slick stuff to me all the time like "Kenny you can't handle this, you would not know what to do with all this, I will have you climbing the wall." I used to laugh and think nothing of what she was saying because she was so silly. Then one day she asked me to pick her up so we could go to this party. In that same sentence Natalie told me that her parents were going to be out of town. That's when it hit me that I needed to take some condoms. After the party we got back to her house and I went in, and the first thing she did was call her boyfriend and tell him that she made it home. Natalie told him that she was about to go to bed, which was true, she just omitted the part about me be in the bed with her. He believed her and said good night.

As I was there at Natalie's house in her room I was thinking are we still going to be able to be friends after this, and was our friendship more important than the sex. And all I could come up with was that the sex was very important. So Natalie and I had sex, the next thing I know she was breaking up with her boyfriend, and I was like whoa, what is that all about? Natalie hit me with some more game and told me that breaking up with him had nothing to do with me. The truth was that I was her prize the whole time. Natalie knew what she wanted when she and I used to flirt in halls and in class. I just fell for the game. The whole time that she was my friend she was just keeping herself close enough to make the move on me. When she had the chance she made the move with sex, something that she and I had talked about so many times. Natalie knew that I wasn't going to turn down the chance to sleep with her. I have to admit I probably always wanted to sleep with her too. I just figured we were friends and I accepted that it wasn't going to happen. Natalie didn't accept that and she did not stop until she made me her man. The break up really was only about me. She used that to keep me even closer and I start spending less time with my girl and more time with her. Natalie would tell me that she just needed someone to hang with, and we had already had sex, so we had sex most times we hung out. She and I actually kicked it for a few months as a couple. Never did I think that she was gaming me and that it was all a set up to get what she wanted. Ladies know the power they have between their legs and will use that in the end to get what they want. We have to be smart enough not to fall into their trap, because now when I look back I miss her more than I do the sex, she was a real friend, now we don't even talk. Who fault is it hers or mine? Is it mine for falling for the game or Natalie's for playing the game? That question really can't be answered, because if she never asked me to come in her house that night would we still have eventfully had sex? We probably would have still had sex, and I would be writing a similar story with the same ending.

My next friend that ran game on me, let's call her Talisha. Talisha was around for a long time. She and I were friends for like seven years. The way it started was we had a lunch together every day when I was in the tenth grade and it was basically because she and I were the only people in our circle that had first lunch. First lunch was the worst lunch to have in school, I remember you would try to change your schedule just so you could have third lunch. Third lunch was like a party, first lunch was like going to dinner with you great grandparents. Talisha and I started to talk about her boyfriends my girlfriends, before long we knew a lot about each other. Talisha's game was a little different; a new approach. Talisha would listen to me talk about my females, and would only say nice things until she felt they became a threat to our friendship. I never noticed the things that she would say, and how she would slide them in or what they really meant. Like when my first love and I got serious in our relationship, me and my first love would argue a lot and I would come to Talisha and ask for advice. Everything she would say would lead me to believe that my girlfriend was doing something wrong. Talisha wanted to keep me just close enough to her so that we could be together someday. Talisha also did what it took to keep me there. Before I hooked her up with one of my friends she and I had already kissed and spent the night together, but that was as far as it went, we were always just "friends". I have to admit she had intrigued me.

I remember one time I was out of town and I told her that I wanted to come see her. And she said cool, I had a few of my friends with me and she said bring them. Once I got to her house one of Talisha's friends invited me to her room right in front of her. I was like hell yeah. So Talisha and I talked for a little while, then I was like I'm about to go upstairs and see what your friend is talking about. Talisha tried to throw salt first she was like "you don't want to go up there she is a whore". I was thinking that's even better for me I don't want a relationship with her any way. Talisha would not let me go, she held onto me tight and pulled me on top of her and said you are sleeping with me. I was like why? Talisha said "I can't have you sleep with one of my friends I may not want you anymore". It was a shock that Talisha was so honest when she said that, but it was the truth, and the truth is all I needed to hear. If she wouldn't have said that I would have still went upstairs, but because she was so honest I chilled. Talisha and I just slept together like we had done so many times and nothing happened as usual. A few kisses, a few hugs and touches, but no real sex. That was a whole new game. That was honest game; she kept it so real with me that I had to chill and just lay with her. My friend had dated her like a year earlier and that made me feel some kind of way about what she was saying. I wasn't thinking right, I wasn't looking at the friendship that Talisha and I had built over the past six years, I was thinking what if.

A week later Talisha came to Charlotte and told me that she wanted to see me, I said cool. She stopped by my house around about eleven, I remember sitting on the couch and watching sports center. Talisha walked directly in my room, then she came back to the door in just a bra and panties. Talisha had the nerve to ask if I was coming to bed . . . . Hell yeah I was going! We did it all night long and it was wonderful while I was having sex with her, but when it was over I laid there feeling so bad for my friend and for my friendship. She caught me so off guard, I thought she was just coming to spend the night like she normally would. She knew what she wanted and she knew what time it was. I fell for the bait, just like a sucker. Talisha had ran her game on me and made me want her. I played back the time I stopped by her house and she would not let me have sex with her friend. I thought about when she told me that she wanted me for herself, and I also remembered when she came to the door half naked. I felt so bad, but it felt so good. She was always so sexy to me, but we were friends, I did have my thoughts, but they were just that; thoughts. Talisha put more thoughts in my head and those thoughts consumed me when the time came to have sex and all of my ability to reason was gone. All I can really say is that she really knew what she was doing and I was a sucker for her game.

I should have known that it was just a little bit more because a few days later she called and asked if I had told my friend what she and I did. And I had, but I hadn't. He and I were riding in the car one day and I told him that I had sex with Talisha and that it wasn't good. And he said well if you would have had sex with her I know that it would have been good, so I know you didn't. So I left it alone, and let him think what he wanted. I felt so bad that I did it, even though it had been years since they were together. I caught a conscience and I couldn't do it any more. I stopped calling Talisha, and about two weeks went by and she called me cursed me out, Talisha said, "Kenny you know me better than anybody, and you know that you can't just have sex with me and not call me!" I apologized and told her that I wasn't feeling right pursuing that type of relationship any more. I have to admit it was really hard for me to say that because the sex was so damn good and we had been close friends for like seven years. I stepped up and cut it off. At least I tried too. My heart still loved her like a friend so it was so hard for me not to want to see her.

Talisha really wanted me to tell him what she and I had did just to make her ex-boyfriend jealous. She went after me and kept me close. I was the penis in the glass, break in case of emergency. Fellas all of you have had friend girls that have flirted with you, and maybe even kissed you now and then. You are their security blanket. When they are lonely you are there, when they want someone to hold them you are there. That's their game. You meet all their boyfriends and they call you their best friend. They are steady telling their boyfriend that they would never do anything with you. Trust and believe you all will have sex one day. All you have to do is hang around long enough. What you have to do to combat that game is find a chick and get real serious with the girl. Make sure you tell your friend girl all about it. If she says mean things about the girl then you know that she wants you for more than just a friend, if she chills and lets you be, she wants you for more than a friend. Either way you are going to get it.

Talisha always wanted me. She would tell me things like I was her type more so than her boyfriends. Her mom and I were really close friends. Hell, her mom would call me sometimes just to talk to me. To say that everything that Talisha did was game may be exaggerating a little bit. When I think back she had no reason to kiss me, she had no reason to let me touch her wherever I wanted. Talisha allowed me to do what I wanted to keep me there. I remember meeting her boy friends and she would tell me that she didn't even like them like that. I also can remember her calling me and telling me how hurt she was, and her crying to me. Those are the things that probably weren't game. It turned out that her pain was so deep that she still wanted payback for the hurt that my friend had caused her years before. In the end she used me to get that payback. There really was no reason for her to ever tell him what we did, especially since I wasn't even going to pursue anything with her. Women are like elephants; they will never forget. Once again that shows you how women move. They are going to make you hurt worst than you ever made them.

To this day I hate that I ever had sex with Talisha, it ruined our whole friendship and she was a true friend. Talisha came and chilled with me when I had chicken pox my senior year. She would come get me and take me places when I didn't have a car, she talked to me everyday about whatever was on my mind and what ever I was feeling. I can say that she is one of the few females that I was completely open and honest with.

Talisha was a friend at least I thought so but the truth is she saw something in me she liked and she kept me close enough to use me for what she wanted at the right time.

My last friend girl I really can't say that she was my best friend, but I can say that whenever we saw each other we could talk for hours like we saw each other all the time. I had a crush on her since we were like five. We are going to call her Emily. Emily and I were in junior high together. At a school dance I remember wanting to dance with Emily all night. I finally got up enough courage to ask her and she danced with me. I wanted to kiss her that night and I thought she wanted to kiss me but I wasn't real enough then to ask for what I wanted. We went all through high school riding to school together, we talked every day and we became pretty close. I remember when some crazy stuff had gone down with her boyfriend and I was torn between telling her or keeping it to myself. Since Emily was my friend, I told her what it was. The sad thing was that Emily did not believe me, and telling her caused tension between us. She didn't talk to me for like three days. Then one day after school Emily came up to me and told me that she was sorry that she did not believe me, and she cried like a baby on the way home from school that day. I always had a feeling that she felt some kind of way about me, but neither of us pursued it. We went through college and chilled together a lot then we lost touch for a while. Every time I saw her she and I could talk like we had just seen each other. Long story short, I was about to get married and I went to see Emily one night before I got married. While I was at Emily's house my friend put us in the room together and locked the door. She laughed and I laughed, then she said something to me that made me think, Emily asked "do you really want to get married?" I was like "yeah I love her."

Emily then said "I can't believe it, I can't believe that you are getting married. I never thought I would see the day that you get married." I left that day and I didn't think anything of what Emily had said. I just figured that she meant since we had been friends for so long that she did not think that I would ever get married.

Once I got married she use to call me all the time about whatever, and she and I had never talked like that before. I remember one time she came over to the house so I could make her a CD. Emily was always silly, and so she was laughing at everything I said. My wife was so mad when Emily left. My wife said, "That girl wants you." I said, "no baby we just cool, we have been cool since junior high." My Wife straight up told me, "no she wants you and I don't want you hanging with her." I kind of cut ties with Emily for a minute, until my wife and I separated. I called Emily to talk and she was so supportive of me, but really negative to my marriage, Emily was like, "I knew she was trouble from the beginning". I have to admit that it was probably my fault for even sharing personal information with an outsider, but I was still under the impression that Emily was my friend and would be objective, never would I have thought that she had her own agenda. She played me to the fullest and took everything I was said and amplified it to make it seem so much worse. That really worked, because my wife and I already didn't trust each other so she just made me think that everything was a lie.

Next thing I know Emily and I started meeting for lunch about three times a week and I was going over her house few times a week too. I was already seeing this other female that was full of game. A lot my nights I spent with my other girl, and Emily hated her, she would just hate, hate, hate on everything about her and that's when I knew Emily wanted me to be more than just her friend. I remember one night I went over to Emily's and she had on the smallest shorts in the world with no panties on, I was like wow. Emily laid her head right on my lap because she loved for me to play in her hair. I told Emily, "you are going to make me play in something else with those little shorts on around me." Emily laughed. So I slowly slid my hand down to that part of her booty that was out and she didn't stop me or ask any questions. All fellas know you have to do the test to see you will be stopped. You slowly, kiss on the neck, touch a breast, or grab their booty or something. If they say nothing then you keep going, if they say stop in a playful way, you keep going, if they so no in a playful way, you keep going. Not all no's and stop's mean stop. Make sure you know the difference; I don't want anyone catching charges and then trying to get off by bringing my book to your trial . . . but back to the story. I turned her over and we kissed like I have never kissed before, I kissed all over her, but she stopped me and said that she couldn't do this. I was like wow because I just knew she wanted to, maybe I was wrong. It was all game, she held out on giving me some because of what she really wanted. I found out what she really wanted the next day. She called me and told me that she couldn't do it because of the fact that I was messing with someone else. I told Emily that the other girl and I were not even like that; we were just having fun. Emily and I went out one night and we got a little drunk, my phone was blowing up from my other girl. I kept telling Emily that I was going to drop her off and go get me some from my other girl. Emily told me "no we are having sex tonight." I was like, "whatever I'm going to see my girl." I remember that night when I got Emily home she told me to walk her to the door, then she told me to come in for a second, then she asked me to lay with her. I kind of didn't want too, but I did because I had liked her so much back in the day. So she and I had sex, it was great, it was wonderful and it was a mistake. I looked at it as if it was just sex, but she looked at it as the start of a relationship. She thought she had gamed me enough for me to let all of my people go and just be with her. I couldn't, because I really did care for the other female I was seeing already, and I cared for Emily too. So what Emily did was use my friend to get back at me. She started messing with him, so I could see him and her together. That just made it easier for me to stay with the female I was with. I still would go see Emily and spend the night with her. We still had lunch, and everything. I looked at us as friends with benefits, good benefits. I think the thing that really killed Emily was that we had a birthday party for her at my house and my girl was there. Emily saw how my girl and I interacted and she did not like that at all. The next day she called me crying, telling me that no one had hurt her like I had, and I felt bad, but it had to be game, hell she and I only had sex for like two months before we realized that we were not going to be able to be a couple. How could I hurt her more than her boyfriends that she spent years with? But then as I thought about it, I knew her from when we were five years old, we talked all the time, I knew most of her personal business and she knew mine, it wasn't about the sexual relationship, it was the fact that she looked at me as someone that she loved and would never hurt her.

Emily was a really good friend, and I loved her as a friend, but we took it to a level that we should not have. I remember her laugh and I remember how we could just laugh about nothing at all, and we used to hang out, and how she would cry in my arms. I miss those things; I miss my friend.

All of my friend girls had their own reason for keeping me around or trying to be with me. Natalie, Talisha and Emily all were close to me, probably too close, and that is why I ended up sleep with each one of them. Natalie knew what she was doing when she was flirting with me all the time and telling me how good she could sex me. Talisha knew what she was doing when she would kiss me, spend the night with me and let me touch her all over. Emily knew what she was doing when she would talk shit about my wife and my girls. Emily really knew what she was doing when she came around me in those little shorts. I guess this answers that age-old question can men and women be friends. I don't really know the true answer but I know it never really worked for me. My problem was that I have never had an ugly woman friend. Maybe if I find an ugly woman to be my friend, and she can't have a body either because you all know we will hit an ugly girl with a sexy body, then maybe our friendship will last. I never came on to either one of my friends, I may have flirted but I wasn't anything like I am with girls that I just meet. I was close enough to all of them that they could use me for whatever they wanted, and it all came down to sex. Sex was their weapon of choice and I was the firing range, now I'm full of bullet holes, and emptiness without them.

# Chapter 11

## "I Love You"

Love is a word that you really shouldn't throw around when you really don't mean it. Love is the reason that we live, love for our children, family, and friends. Love should not be used in your games or to get what you want from someone. Females sometimes use that as a last resort. Like if you are about to walk out the door, they yell "you can't leave me, I love you". Even if you leave out of the house that day the fact that she told you that she loves you will stay on your mind, and sometimes that will make you come back and try to work it out with them. They may not even really love you they just don't want to be alone.

I remember this one girl I was kicking it with for about a month was doing every single thing I wanted. She was probably the perfect girl, but I was not feeling her at all. When I told her that it was over the first thing she said to me was that she loved me. Now she had said it to me before and I ignored it. I think her saying that she loved me was what really led me to say that it was over. At point she felt that she had done so much for me she just couldn't let me go that easy. Although she and I had only kicked it for a couple of months she was trying to make me feel certain that she loved me. She was trying to use the 'I love you card' as her game, when that should never be a game. Needless to say it didn't work, I still left.

Fellas have to watch out for the females that say I love you quickly. A lot of that is all game, sometimes with certain people you know that they really have love for you but they don't love you. Although some females are looking for that pity love, they say I love you and you feel compelled to say it back. They say I love you, just so if you all ever fought, they could always say I thought you loved me. It's a game. Don't fall victim. I fell victim to the word love. Hell, I loved back for real, but for her it was all a game.

The truth in loving someone is that there are different levels of love. You love people where you don't want to hurt them, but then you love people where you won't hurt them. Let me dig a little deeper so you all can feel what I'm saying. I have been in the middle of both loves, my first love, loved me with all her heart and soul, but she still didn't love me enough not to want to hurt me. The real love is when you think of your significant other before you are willing to make a move. So to all my fellas I'm here to help yall decipher what love you have. If your women tells you that she is going out with her girls and will see you later, or just to call her tomorrow when you wake up, and finish the statement with I love you bay, then she may love you, but she is not opposed to hurting you. Now if your girl tells you my girls called and they wanted me to go out with them tonight but I told them that I'm hanging with my baby. You have that real love. Love can come and go. Ya'll know how when you first start in a relationship and it starts getting serious and you would rather be around them, all the time. Ya'll know like when you call them they always answer the phone for you no matter what they are doing. And if they don't answer the phone, when they call you back they say, I'm sorry baby I was doing such and such and couldn't come to the phone. You get that apology and you get the reason why they didn't answer the phone, because they care and they want to make sure that the relationship moves along without any hiccups. The truth be told my parents has been together for almost 40 years and never, not once have I heard them say I need some me time, I just need to get away and hang with my friends. Real love don't need getaways. Some of ya'll reading this now saying one of two things, damn do I really love the person I'm with or this dude don't know what he is talking about. The ones that think I don't know what I'm talking about don't love the person they are with, or they are just denying the signs that their girl doesn't love them.

Women use that I love you word loosely, and they use it to their advantage, when they ask you to buy them something they end it with I love you. When they ask can you take them somewhere they end it with I love you. When they get off the phone from lying to you they end it with I love you. My second Love I had that type of love for her that if I wasn't going out with her I had no reason to go out. It was to my surprise that she didn't share that same type of love for me. All men have women like her in their life, or that passes through their life to teach them a valuable lesson. She was caught in three lives, she had a baby daddy that she loved, she had me that she showed that she loved and she had a life that she had not experienced yet. Notice that I said that she showed that she loved. Her problem was she had nowhere to go. A woman with nowhere to go becomes creative, women will lean on what they know to get to where they need to get to. Women will do everything that you like when they don't have options. They will cook for you, clean for you, have sex the way u like it, they will be that strong mother figure to your children, what ever it takes to show their love, or said love. And we as fellas eat it up, and we never pick up on the small things that will tell us that this is not real love that she is showing me love to benefit her. Fellas are so stubborn and bull headed we believe that we got it going on like no other, and there is no way in the world that she is faking this love. The little things we miss out on is the fact that once or twice a week she is begging you for money to go hang out with her friends, she always encourages you to go out with your friends, every time you start feeling some kind of way about something that she is doing she always tell you that she loves you. The random "I love Yous'" are a wonderful thing, but "I love yous'" to stop you from asking question or feeling some kind of way about what they are doing is the I love you that you do not want to hear. My second love that's what I was to her, a stepping stone, until she was able to provide for herself as long as she needed me in some way shape or form she would do what ever I asked of her. The minute that she had found her own way through life is when I got her ass to kiss. When she was there with me she made me feel like a king, what ever I wanted what ever I liked she did, and if we would ever fight it was sex then a million I love yous, just to keep me loving her. Then she was right back doing everything it took to prove her love, the easy and truthful thing would have been to just say hey you know I don't feel like you feel about me and I really wont to see other people. She knew by saying that, she and I would be finish and she still needed me to take care of her, so she shot me phony love, its funny I use to tell her all the time, that all her hugs and love was fake the only really love I got from her was from her daughter, her hugs and kisses was real love, but children always give real love. That's what women do, I asked my study group and they all said the same thing, that if they fell out of love with a dude, before they tell him that they don't love him they are going to make sure they have everything in order so if push comes to shove they will have somewhere to go. My question to them was why wouldn't you just ask to stay until then? They all agreed that it would be out of fear of him kicking them out, not loving them anymore, or they was just being selfish. They said they would continue to go on like everything is perfect because they don't want to hurt his feelings and plus they have to make sure they really don't love him any more. I told them that is game, they tried to disagree but any time that you are not being honest for an arterial motive, you become the person that is running game and playing a game where there is no winner. She used me to get where she felt she needed to get in life it was I love you every single day until she had her own.

Love comes and goes, people fall in and out of love but true love endures forever. Women using I love you is not always their fought but it is always a game. What happens sometimes is that the man has hurt the women so bad that now she has fell so far out of love there is not any way they can go back to having real love for him. What women should say is that I don't love you any more instead of still saying that they love you knowing that they are out there trying to find what they thought was real love again. Once the trust is broken in any relationship it takes an act of God to bring her feelings back. What we do as fellas is we get so comfortable because at one time she did have real love for you, the type of love where she would rather be with you then to be out with her friends, even if she went out with her friends it was cool for you to come to. The type of love where she answer the phone on the first ring, and if she don't, she apologizes and give the reason why she didn't answer, but not any more. Now she tells you that she is going out with her friends and she will call you later that night or tomorrow, and if she live with you she becomes real disrespectful coming in at five or six in the morning, but before she wasn't like this. Now us as fellas get all suspicious and self conscience because now when you call she take forever to answer if she even answers. When she calls you back its not like before you can sit on the phone for 10 minutes and you wont get an apology, you wont get a reason, you will have to ask why she didn't answer the phone 9 hours ago when you called her 20 times in a row. All she will say is that my phone was in the car, I was sleep, I didn't see that you called, I love you baby stop tripping. So now we are the insecure man that no woman wants she got us going crazy wondering why things have changed so much. When she is asleep we are trying to get on your phone so we can go through her messages and Facebook all because we messed up and now we are worried about what she is doing. She continued to tell you that she loves u all the time, and every time before she goes out with her girls she tells you that she loves you. We as fellas are so stupid that her saying I love you put our mind at ease, and we think she isn't going to do anything to hurt us. Fellas we give them a pass because we feel like they wouldn't hurt us but the fact of the matter is the old them would not hurt us. The female that we have changed them into could care less how we feel about what happens. Like when I drove my first love to that point everything started to change. When she had real love for me she wouldn't smoke cigarettes around me because I didn't like smoke, when she fell out of love with me she would light up and blow the smoke right in my face. Then she started dressing up just to go to the store. I would say do you have to get as fly as you can, all we need is some bread. It wasn't about me any more it was about what ever she needed to do to make her self feel better. She kept telling me that she loved me to make me feel better about what was obviously going on right in front of my eyes. That "I love you" game kept me guessing kept me thinking that maybe we had a chance to work it out.

What we as fellas have to do is watch the change in your girl, or watch what they do from the beginning of a relationship. Once those words I love you are said you can tell if someone loves you for real or if the love they are talking about is, I love you when we are together, but when we are not its all about me. True love is when you can put someone's feelings before your own, you make decisions for the both of you and not just what you want to do. Females are so good at what they do now a days to pull the wool over our eyes and we believe that the love that they are giving us is unconditional and that love that we feel seem so real. We start to follow our heart and they are following their wants. Some only want to be independent, some only want, not to love you any more, some just don't want you to leave but the way they go about it is all game. Once that trust is gone from either party then the games begin, we as fellas are playing a game that we can't win. The truth would be nice, but the truth would be to easy, so females string you alone make you feel that they still love you, or make you feel like they forgive you for what has happen but the real truth is that they don't wont anything else to do with you they are just playing the game because aint nothing else to do. They don't have another person to love, they don't have anywhere else to go, or they just going to keep living the life that you are providing them, but now they are going to do their own thing. If we miss out on the signs, and the difference in the I love yous, then we will get played, but its not really an argument we all know that women have more game then men, the problem is we fail to recognize the signs when game is getting ran on us.

# Chapter 12

# No More Games

We would love to think that every one was honest, and that everything that we did was what we really wanted to do. So people call making sacrifices for a relationship "compromising", but when you compromise who you are, it turns into game. I have to admit that I've had a very interesting life, and I have seen women play their boyfriends with me, play me with other guys, make me love them, and use me for personal gain. A lot of the time I was only in it because of what I was getting out of it, and sometimes living in that second life led me to think and feel that it was more than what it actually was. Game is really the choice that you make to be honest with someone, or lead them to believe something other than the truth. Having game helps you pep game, and recognize phony people. Once your heart is open to someone you soon forget all of the lies and the games they were shooting from the start. Love is that one blind spot in the review mirror. It will have you crossing lanes when the road really isn't clear, and you never see it coming.

How do you really say no to a female that will do whatever you want? Women know that a man can't say no and that is how they run game. It starts from the very beginning when they use their terms of endearment, like Baby, Sexy, Cutie, and Babe; it makes you feel like you are a little more to them. The truth is that you are not their baby, they just want you to feel like they are really into you. That's all a part of their game. Then they will tell you that they love you when they really don't. Women will tell you that you are their best when their last man was their best too. Then females believe in revenge, and they believe in letting you find out about it. Women aren't going to do a lot of people to get you back; they are going to do the one person that they know will hurt you the most. Women will tell you they love you, to make you stay, to try and make you love them, or just to confuse you to what's really going on. When a lot of times they see something that they want, they foresee you as the person that they can spend the rest of their life with so they do what they have to do to make you love them.

I know that I have told you all a lot about myself. I feel like I have just as much game as females but the truth is nobody knows everything. My only problem has been that I always love the wrong female. I know for a fact that my first love really loved me with all her heart, her problem was that she didn't trust me. The fact that I was never home played with her mind and made her think the worst of me. I was a good man until I found out that she was cheating on me. Once I found that out I went back to who I was when she and I first started, maybe that was who I always was and I was just trying to be something else. My first love showed me game from a different level, I always thought game was words. She was able to show me game was the words that were never spoken. As far as my second love, for me to say that she never loved me and only used me to get to where she wanted to be in life, may be a stretch. I believe that she had deep feelings for me, but they never reached the depths of her love for herself. My first love showed me that there are women out there that are just like me. We would sit in the car and laugh at each other answer questions, because we both knew the other one was bullshitting. She pepped game and I did too. That was so strange and appealing at the same time, because of what and who I thought she was I fell in love. My second love used that to kill my thoughts of love.

Through out my life all of the women that I have messed with, have been associated with, and been friends with, have shown me that women don't sit back any more and allow men to run game on them. Most women are one step ahead of their man. A woman can have a good idea that their man is cheating on them two weeks before they even say anything to them. A woman will always know the score of the game even when you are hiding the stat sheet. They will always know if they should cheat, if they should trust you and if they need to make you love them. That is how women gage their game and how they are going to manipulate the relationship. The easiest thing that we can say is "no more games" but the truth is that the games will never stop. The key is knowing when it's real or when it's fake. I can tell you this; it's much easier said than done. The only way to have a straight up relationship is by having equal trust between the man and woman. Most women have been bruised by pervious relationships, and men won't admit it, but they have been bruised too. So can we live in a world where everyone is honest, where we do what we say and what we say we do? Yes but no, because there's no way that everyone is going to trust, and there's no way that we can get the man and the woman to both agree to "no more games."